Gary the Thief/Gary Upright

By the same author

Poems

Don't Exaggerate
The Breath of the Crowd

Plays

Claw
The Love of a Good Man
Fair Slaughter
That Good Between Us
The Hang of the Gaol
The Loud Boy's Life
Crimes in Hot Countries
Downchild
No End of Blame
Victory
The Power of the Dog
A Passion in Six Days
Scenes from an Execution
The Castle
Women Beware Women
The Bite of the Night
The Possibilities
The Europeans

Film

The Blow

Howard Barker

Gary the Thief/Gary Upright

JOHN CALDER : LONDON
RIVERRUN PRESS : NEW YORK

First published in Great Britain, 1987, by
 John Calder (Publishers) Ltd.,
 18, Brewer Street, London W1R 4AS

and in the United States of America, 1987, by
 Riverrun Press Inc
 1170 Broadway
 New York, NY 10010

British Library Cataloguing in Publication Data

Barker, Howard
 Gary the thief/Gary upright
 1. Title
 821'.914   PR6052.A6485
 ISBN 0 7145 4137 0

Printed in Great Britain by Delta Press, Hove.
Typeset in Baskerville by Oxford University Computing Service.

For
Ian McDiarmid

Contents

Gary the Thief	1
Gary Upright	21
Plevna	39
I Repeat Myself	64
This at Least	66
Lend the Poor an Enemy	67
We Are Losing, So ...	68
The Dance of Two Coolies	71
When We Burned the Scientist	76
At Least It Was Evil	78
A Rebuke to the Socialist David Blunkett	80
Rare Visitor	81
Factory Store	82
A First Lullaby for the Impatient	83
The Effect of Dancers on Poets	85
To the Aberystwyth Students	87

Gary the Thief

Oh, you monkeys
I the thief
Piss over you

Oh, you cattle
I suck your udders
The weasel in the moonlight
Rising on hind feet

Gary the thief
Glimpsing senility totter to its den
His inturned foot
Mimicking age's friction with the ground
Tracked along the broad band of its scent
This bonebag of unwritten history

Oh, its odour
Oh, its self-neglect
Its stained tapestry
Of shags
    mournings
    bombs
    and landlords
Its bruised skin
And inflamed eye

Oh, die
Oh, die
I hate the weak
And whimper in the presence
Of the strong

Gary the thief

You monkeys
You cattle
I tread your consciences like a brass heeled
Titan wades a sea of eggs

2

In the mirror
Seeing himself seen
The barely audible throb of a baby
Unfathoming eyes
Uneducated fingers
He ceased rifling

Gary the thief

His deft intrusions
His quaking of humble order
His swivelling eye sweeping
The seams of poverty
Are seized in its liquid stare

And
In
The
Pause

He experiences the rise of infamy
The garlands of public hate
Which hoarse headlines will in only hours
Drape his narrow shoulders with

Gary the thief

With a single swipe
Bursts perception's grasping
Soddens light

The echoing basin drains to silence

One yell less of neglect
One mouth less of hunger
One throat less to approve

Aren't babies cheap
His sister had six
Aren't babies old men
They get under his feet
And in its way it was impertinent
In its way it reproved him

I live among you
Hating you

I eat your flanks
Smiling

I charm you
With the ease of one who holds
All effort in contempt

Gary the thief

Wears murder like a brooch

Your joy's my peach

The arrest of Gary the thief

Its conviviality
Its swap of sour humour
Its dispensing with the
Paraphernalia of the police

He goes quietly
In case a moral idiot should brand his cheek
He is the soul of apology
In case a zealot should crack his teeth

The teeming tears of his mother
The showering sobs of the occasional wife
Play him down the lift
As bands bray to parting regiments

And seeing the rolling up
Of the familiar street
He wishes on his neighbours

> Excruciating death
> Blind babies
> Gas escapes and
> The subsequent collapse of flats

Gary the thief

His captors in the hurtling van
Already applaud his wit

They laugh
They clap
They Gary this and Gary that

       Cigarette son

     Chewing gum

        Play yer cards right

     Guard yer bum

And to the cells he marches dignified as the
Plenipotentiary of powers momentarily overcome

4

Somewhere the unkindness recurs
Always recurs

Poor diet in the seventh month
The angle of the birth
Exposure to fumes in the pram
The way the mother bawls
The shards from damaged throats
A shrapnel of abuse
Through which the infant crawls

This made Gary the thief

Or if you refuse
Chalk morality on the high walls
Spray free will on the corrugated fence
Which flaps its admonitions at the balconies

But he disdains the damaged character as cause

My defence lies in your opulence
Says Gary the thief
Your greed dwarfs my offence
Your violence staggers the ropes of the globe
The very sandwich which the warder bites
Was yanked from in between the jaws
Of children thin as kites

I am only
I am simply
I am the crow of the city
Silently descending

Am I not the swift-handed interpreter of the
Governing Principle?

And with the pale mouth of one
Who stumbled upon eloquence
As the lonely bachelor stuffed
The drifted knickers underneath his coat

> Appropriating mystery
> Breathless with success
> And for the absent truth erect

He looked from eye to faltering eye

You monkeys
You cattle

I pilfer your language
I pilfer your respect

Prison

Its revocation of fellowship
Its playing for advantages
And the dirty glamour attaching to
Insane and paltry acts

How its order favoured him

Gary the thief

He tatooed patriotic symbols on his palms
Verso a profile of the Pope
He kissed where strength insisted
Confining pride to the memory
And his eyes withdrew to the sockets' deeps
As animals hibernate the winter
Uninjured by the stabbing of persistent light

Gary the thief

Does not degenerate
Or shed himself in tempers
And behold

These hinges and these bolts are pure lard
These cameras and these levered locks run fluid
In the combustion of the state

You mugs
You morons
I walk through the prostrated gate
To my first amnesty

Son of the Revolution

6

Let us recognize in Gary
The party theorist says
An ally of the revolution
Whose misplaced zeal
Demonstrates the squandered
Initiative of the oppressed

Reclaim him

How preferable he is to
Intellectuals or priests

The District Organizer shares his bed
And encourages him to
Weave out of old hates
A proper class analysis

He yawns in the debates
And slips his finger down her jeans

She was posh once
She was immaculate
And now signs labour drafts
And orders throwing snobs into the street

Gary the thief

She extracts a secret pleasure
From his elegance

Gary the thief

The monkeys
The cattle

I ride History lightly as a leaf
On torrents which wash away the
Gates of prisons and of parks

7

And was put in authority

Gary the thief

Was made responsible
According to the theory that
The contemptuous harbour love
Only at depth

Love whose tender wings are damply folded
In the carapace of scorn
Which trust would crack
As sunshine thaws the chrysalis

So in his hands they poured

     The clay of poets
     The putty of professors
     The wax of idealists

For him to mould

Gary the thief

Team leader and
Reformer of parasites

You bastards
You snobs

I piss on your secrets
I tear your long words into shreds
And watch hard labour
Break the fine threads
Of carefully spun privacies

STAND BY YOUR BEDS

8

Lying beside her in the pulped night
The hours until dawn densely queuing
Her body meat without taste
Her limbs undemocratically annexing
His sheet
His mattress

Gary the thief

Experienced the plunge of mortal horror
Some time between 3 and 4 a.m.

And
    fell
        incessant
            fall

Through
        every
           net
              of
                habit
                    fiction
                        or
                        relief

His terror finding no holds in malice
His wit throwing no clasps
His cunning failing to catch
And his unreflected self
Drilled and blown like the egg
Of the extinct breed on the museum shelf
All brittleness and dispersed possibility

Gary the robbed

Scrambles into his suit
And wakes the duty sergeant for the key
To the hut where the intellectual criminals
Toss on rusty bunks

WAKE UP IT'S ME

You impostors
You one-time seducers of gullible girls

Get up and fix infinity

9

He shivers

A greasy vellum stretched on wires

He rocks

The parasite whose toothless diction mocks
Profundity

And soon dawn laps the sacks which hang as blinds

OH, CHRIST I HAVE TO DIG AT FIVE

Visioning the eighty baskets he must shift of beet
And frost which turns the furrow knife to feet

No, persevere
Who's Ockham
Come again

And this Duns Scotus with the barmy name
Abbreviate him
How did they squirm from underneath the
Suffocating sheet?

But stubbornly he only stares
A cavernous and unrepentant mouth

Gary would filch the learning by the ear
Or draw it like a strand of silk
Through the dead pupils of his eyes

SPEAK

You hoarder of knowledge
Pain's profiteer

I will lever
I will prise
The floorboards of your brain
As once I stove in the locks of paltry cabinets

10

Gary the thief
Keeps the brain in a jar

It sits on the shelf
It blindly stirs to his tilting

Is this the fungus conscience creeps among
Slow as the beetle in the bark?

Is this the suet desire boils
In the skull's basin?

The pulp of calculation?
Hatred's grey mounds
And the grooves of kindness?

He shakes it violently
As if to separate base urges from the wisdom

He cradles it on his pillow
As if its silence would succumb to passion

I Gary the thief
Who learned nothing
Not even the paucity of education

I coax
I murmur
I entice

The power not of thought
That you can keep

But of ceasing to think
The shutting down of imagination

That brings sleep
To Gary the thief

11

They cross the field in a stooping line
The charges of Gary the thief
The bovine cough in the fog
And the clang of the short-bladed knife

Oiled water sits stagnant in the levels
And the trees give nothing

They give nothing yet
To Gary the dispossessed

The baskets move to the checker
And move away again
The reverberation of the beet
Falling to the floor of the bin

A woman moves in a window
The jerks of the curtain signal nothing

They signal nothing yet
To Gary the dispossessed

He makes his mouth an orange of abuse
Vivid
Succulent
More acid than the prisoners dreamt

Who pities the overseer
His struggle with excess?
Who feels the interrogator's
Tumour of contempt?

Then
      most
           unpolitically
                he
                    kneels

And breathes a request

If I do not inspire fear
If I do not

What am I?

Tell me what

They stare from eyes half blind
Eyes simply functional
Still as cattle disturbed
And none lends him a word
None tosses him the gnawed bone of a word

The wind
The shame
Make his eyes smart

His laugh
His bark
Is jagged as the saw in the timber's heart

Only a trick
You
Only a trick

12

The burial of the brain
Its secret place beneath the beech

He recites

    I Gary of Harmony Farm
    Trepanned a criminal professor
    Subsequent to his decease
    I did this for knowledge
    But nothing came of it
    God or whatever give him peace

And kicking the deep moist mould into
A fickle tumulus
Walks towards the perimeter lights

But his mooncast shadow is spiked on the thorn
And ivy snares his boots
He demonstrates no urban swerves
But trips on the unpaved roots

And his laugh

Untuned by cynicism
Unharmonized with wit

His laugh
Is the cruellest note the wood has heard
It hangs to horrify
Like the pole-trapped bird

The laugh of Gary the thief

If clods would only fall like rain
As softly
As benign
He would not exert a muscle
To deflect his covering

13

Morning comes to Gary the thief

The cold has riddled his youth
And the ice has quarried his teeth
The horror has plucked out fistfuls of hair

And his clothes hang in holes
His overseer's hat
A papier mache novelty the wind bowls
Over fences and dykes

I shall go forth and be a prophet
Says Gary Upright

Words will crowd in my mouth
They will queue in my throat
Words shaped by pity or rage
They will press in the wings
And burst like actors flooding a stage

Sometimes they will flow with
The irresistible hush of lava

S,nothering

Sometimes they will be jagged as
The bomb-burst lancets of cathedrals

Cascading

I shall plant my feet in the railway tracks
In the sunken rails of the cranes
While the drunks ascend the ferries
I shall reveal

And the hooded crow will listen
It will cease its pilfering
Ignoring the rushing of chains
The grinding of the wheel
It will stand on one leg
And its eye will mirror the pains
Of a life of opportunity

I shall reveal

Gary Upright

I come to you without anger or exaggeration
I proffer myself

I present myself without the usual hush
Attaching to the voices of the saved

And clean shaven
So as not to threaten you with hair

I will teach you how to live and die alone
I will make you this gift free of charge
Standing here on the broken kerb
Between the police house and the telephone
And the gushing of drains will not complicate
Nor will the endless reversing of cars suffocate
My message

I have a message of course

Pity the man who has no message
And the woman who refrains

Pity the man who finds no madness
And the woman who refrains

Pity us all whose flesh is not the subject
Of campaigns

This incessant fog obscures everything
Except my voice
My voice it magnifies

Booming at the movers of money
And the issuers of writs
The divorce lawyers
The child specialists

I hear their heels
I hear their handbags
Which are caravans of debt
Shh
Their intestinal disorders
And their rashes shedding into vests

I hear you
And you thought you might slip by
You think he is not here yet
The spectre of Gary
He must have overslept

No

It is only the fog's bargain with mischief
Its old dalliance with our hidden self

I'm here as ever
If anything more so
And my text today will be
(Yes, even the illiterate have texts
They especially deny imagination
They especially cannot rely on spontaneity)
Gary chapters 1 to 3

2

My thinness owes nothing to asceticism
Believe me I was equally thin
When practising

My virtuosity owes nothing to study
Vocabulary I found
Lying on the ground

As I found wit and artifice
In the doorways of the suburbs
And even ways of standing to
Discourage men and win women

I narrate disintegration among rulers
And the kindness of the enemy
I report the speed at which fear grips the innovative
And the intolerable loneliness of the habitually free

And watching you will see
I rarely move
Believing the stylites had a point
I refrain from gesture
Thinking it the mark of politicians
And when the rain becomes enraged with me
Concede
Preferring the air vent of the lawcourts where
Exhaled apologies and abject phrases can be
Breathed
And the lungs lacquered in a tar of vehemence

Also I face East
Allowing the setting sun to burn about my head
Igniting stooks of hair
And casting my shadow in the path of workers
While my eyes in a blind stare
Are focussed on a single point arbitrarily selected

In this affect of seizure
I have the attributes of a god unnamed
Which you are also
But since you won't affirm your deity
Since you will smother
Since you will obscure the light with your hand
Observe the practices of one who
Stands before you unashamed

I was a thief
But I will not labour you with private life
I was a murderer
But I will not prod these details in your ear
As the idle finger intrudes litter in upholstery
You lack the patience for biography
Your own included
Least of all your own
Despite the snapshot and the telephone

I forgave myself so long ago
Whole governments ago
Trodden and blood sodden ideologies ago
Forgive yourselves also
You are so hard
You transport punishment even on the wedding floor
You pile up sentences and like the lag
Dread to be cast out the little door
A free woman

3

May I therefore detain you
And undress you with my eyes

It's true I shall be here tomorrow
But oddly I do not repeat myself
What you miss now is perpetual loss
Bereavement
Yes
An absence
So restrain the habit of your knees
Which drive you so corruptly and mechanically on
Do cease
And allow me to expose you to the unkind air
No not for that
Not for the satisfaction of
Oh no I am not of that ilk
Not now
What truth could be extracted from
The proof more nakedness exists
And yet more nakedness exists
Allow me rather strip
The public off your pale tenderness
Madame
And from the scaffolder
Who swinging on his perch
Bawls such mundane abuse
Monsieur

We come into the world not of our own volition
True or false?

The body of the airman plummetted through
Such a diabolical landscape

His own making

The city rose and fell like boiling tar

His own stirring

Here and there things bloomed in fragments
And the cathedral fell like the dying draught animal
Silently between the shafts

He revolved with the agility of gymnasts

Metal passed
Straining with the ascent
Relieved at the apex
Singing in its fall

The intrepid climb of missiles loyally swimming the dark

To witness this the airman lived an ordinary life
To witness this he had been poorly gifted
And kept a wife by knocking on innumerable doors
A seller of insurance who had no clause
Against this act of God

He came into this world not of his own volition yet

Did the two parts of him not plead
Did the two parts not ache
Pressing the flesh into service
Conscripting the separate shapes
And beating them together like pugged clay

Oh further still and do not relent
Uncover her with or without consent
Steer him kindly to the place
Study his disposition in his face
Whisper the little phrases whose banality
Is sanctified by familiarity

And even along the cool marches where
Love is honestly rewritten
All gift
All theft
All pity
And intransigence

It could not be different

The fervent parents
Or the hardly fervent
Are equally the unborn's instruments

The airman striking roofs came immediately apart
The buttons in one direction
The brains in another
Ringing on the cobbles
Seeping down the gutter

Over yards and privvies the navigator rained

The rat manoeuvred the disconnected hand with
The concentration of a looter marching a fridge
The hand which was lightly clenched as
The woman's in the act of love or
The baby fathoming

Kind
Utterly kind

I tell you this
A piece of perfect history
I tell you this
Because you need to know

Not wishing to
Not going out of your way to
Not actively discouraging however

That condition of idleness
One knee across the other
During which the uncontested criminality occurs

The smothering of a democracy
The mutation of a cell in the laboratory
Another act of unfelt love

But equally a disarray might yet be born
In the time it takes the hand to travel
From the ash tray to the yawn

4

I tell the possible
Which must have effects
I never doubted it would have effects

I stand in the wind like this
And I will not go unpunished
I never doubted I would be punished

And the wind tears the words from my mouth
The words today are somewhat oblique
The words are all over the shop

But that is not a reason to desist
One might lodge in the whorl of a salesman's ear
Or in the deep caves of a mother's neck

You must walk slower
While in possession of the power to walk fast

You must remain behind
While possessing the power of flight

Imitating the senile gaoled in immobility
Who wince to hear their infancy sung
In the mouths of the falsely considerate
(*'She understands a lot more than you ...'*)

Imitating the mad compelled to hear reason
Their smiles are the smiles of angels
But they plan such complex revenge
(*'He's not as daft as he pretends ...'*)

This way you may pick up a secret or two

Oh listen
Do you think I am not equally depressed
I am depressed
So depression prone
Though I am planted with the squareness of a windmill
Like a windmill made to sing in the wind
By wind I shall be overthrown

You've only got one life
True or false?

The suicide returned to the country to die
Where he had herded sheep during a war
Where as a child he had found poetry in
An undistinguished landscape
Singing as he came through the dirty village
Love songs to an absent mother

He emptied the room to feel himself better
Piling the furniture outside the door
And on the familiar hour the window pane
With widow's nerves announced the
Log train's mounting of the incline

Nothing had progressed

Its whistle called to the city yards
Its wheels were hardly turning
And his body parted the cool wheat stalks
As a loved boat separates the rushes
The moon attending
He felt he was going up for a prize
And the moon was his mother attending

Something had substituted itself

He lay on the ballast as if it were a shoulder
And his hand held the wrist of the rail
Which trembled pitifully like a struck down brother
Which trembled like a disconsolate brother
Through the tarred timber and the plate
A damaged brother returned by the state

Everything had failed to be necessary

You may have noticed the most absurd occurrences
Which fall within the compass of my eye
Fail to provoke the typical response
For this I must apologise
I know how laughter reassures those
Soon to be seduced

In this refusal I exemplify
The humourless disposition of the heretic
Whose fragile structures are not proof
Against conviviality

He knows laughter only binds us in contempt
He knows laughter's power to diminish
The cynical pretension
The solitary intention

Both

He knows laughter is ambition's wreath

In any case I have no teeth

And at the moment of decision chose not to lie but jump
The usurpation of a second life
Imagination's final cry
Made him decide to jump not lie
And on the timber's back
Bruise to the bruise of naked wood
He knew he might undo the very arches
On which his purpose stood
And make instead low undulating walls
Perfectly unfunctional

Knew he might be unkinder
Less loving
Suffering fewer fools

More leather than sponge
More oak than cork
More slub than lace

Yielding himself only to the subtle woman whose
Worn fingers move reluctantly to the embrace

A shepherd in the city
A fishmonger in a landlocked country
An unfathomable grinder of lenses

5

How long I have stood here
You could not judge
How long on this pavement
Which lorry wheels have milled
You could not hope to guess
I have the sort of tenancy
That trees possess
Whose sapling days are beyond
The urge of memory

Neither a lover of the carnival
Amazed that crowds might sway in unison
Nor him who stands at the rear of the church
Drawing solitariness into the injured lung
I pick the public place to be unpublic in

34

And the sun which brings you rushing
To a nakedness brings bruising to my skin

This is the season I can least tolerate

Imagination lies heat stricken
And the body always was so poor
Even the dancer knows
Standing so poised in the declining light
Her arse proposing more than
She would willingly invite
Even the dancer knows its arguments are thin

You have to die some time
True or false?

Choosing to view injustice as a sickness
Choosing to submit to prison as one concedes
To the authority of the disease
Putting aside all thoughts of escape
And the interventions of jurists
Ceasing to pray for earthquakes
And regarding the amnesty as one might
The mirage dancing in a stranger's eyes

She wiped the memory of innocence from mind

Worked at its oblivion as if with the knuckle
Daily at the granite wall she scrubbed a
Dead man's signature and thus
Was more economical with friction than
The borers of holes and the filers of bars
Whom innocence drove mad
Were they not all innocent in here?
It was a prison for the innocent

And by practice
Which was the only action left to will
By application to a single thought
Imagination having atrophied
By intensity
Since there was no possibility of variety
She stopped her heart whole minutes
Dying over and over again in solitude
And learned that death does not choose us
But is ours to choose

You see the sweat runs down my face
Inevitably
Since I wear my wardrobe in its entirety
Inevitably I appear uncomfortable
In the extravagance of sun
My several waistcoats
My mash of shirts

And fingerless gloves through which
My insensitive ends poke like
The useless barrels of garrison guns

But I am not tired
I am not broken yet

Not yielding to the burster of the little vein
Not yielding yet

Rather it is true we have to live some time

Not only gravity would pull us low
But the philosopher who lives under the stairs

The servers of fictions
The chairmen of factions
The ageing hawkers of perceptions
Keep telling us that we must die

Which I deny
Emphatically deny

Since to accept the power of the obvious
Is only sometimes the mark of the wise

You have gone home
In a rattle of feet
Receding like a flock of starlings
A rising up of a black sheet
At the hand clap of five o'clock

I admit the probability that nothing entered in
But I refined

Imperceptible redefinitions occurred
Which at a later date may seem significant

The rehearsal was a good one I judge

And I will be here tomorrow assuredly
Oh, assuredly

I trust

Plevna
Meditations on Hatred

Along the floor of the ravine
A mattress

And after that an ox picked clean

A wheel

A suitcase of paper money
Issued by the previous regime

The passage of losers

*

Old women at this altitude
Once seated cannot rise

The sheep stare
Their bells are dull to die by

In the morning the shepherd
Will curse this jetsam in the pasture

*

They sleep at any angle
As if dropped from clouds

And dew collecting in the little basins of their eyes
Overflows

*

This one has the Koran stitched to his chest
By knives

The spiked pages
Are noisy as paper windmills in the breeze

2

Who was drowned by the snow
Which rose to the mouth of the sleeping sentry
The thaw will show

The corpse of the horse plunged
In the Black Sea
After its rolling navigation of the Danube

The bridge of boats transported
Gamblers and experts in ethics
To a common draw

In
   battle
       perhaps
            we
               shall
                  discover
                     the
                        nature
                           of
                           our
                              limits

In a way no farm or marriage could instruct us
The peasant feels
The student articulates

Do horses notice the stars
The general enquired of the groom
The carriage yawning

I have never observed a horse gaze up
Or sheep contemplate the moon
Yet they assess risks swifter than we do

The carriage upholstery bore the marks
Of moisture from the crack of his mistress
He would not sponge for worlds

3

All these were killed
Not by the army
But by neighbours
Who in later years
To satisfy the curiosity of children
Talked of the peculiar speed
At which relations deteriorated

Hatred was described as an infection
And murders happened like a rash
Malice was caught
And this plague's grip
Produced such abnormalities as

Ecstasy at suffering
Dancing in the light of burning farms
Maligant expressions disfiguring the kind

The symptoms of a fever
The delirium
Which only murder stilled

But one said
One with a very ordinary eye
Even when smiling I nourished hate under my tongue
Which flooded
An abundant saliva
When politics exposed the fear
In those we lived among

4

The priest marches
The priest bivouacs

Propping his altar on the limber
Picking his psalm from the mud

The hem of his cassock is stained
From the blood of horses
His boots are thick from the hospital floor

He senses
       pity atrophy
       charity diminish
       and faith's suffocation
       in the odour of the stump

If only he could blind himself with blood
And call the maimed God's netted shoal

If only he could live a leech on pure pain
Tasting the wound
Hearing the nerve
Witnessing the convulsion of the brain

But suffering is too vehement

It will direct the eye
It will command the conscience
It will insist on reasons with its rasp

Oh, the relief with which at last
He lays aside the burden of impartiality

Finding hate so simply
Finding also, sleep

5

The emperor witnessed the decimation
From a platform made of planks
Equipped with an elevated seat

Beside him a number of cordials
                a number of generals
                an awning to ward off the Balkan heat

At 3 p.m. the bombardment ceased

The qualified
The ineducable
The victims of social malformation
The triumphers over circumstances
The sires of revolutionaries
The guardians of racketeers
The inveterately servile
The habitually insolent
The sexually deviant
The attenders at life class
The wife beaters
The horse blinders
The over-considerate lovers
The tamers of birds
The eczematic
The asthmatic

In clean linen
Sockless or
In bare feet

Ran towards the entrenched enemies of Christ

The impalers of infants
The farmers of the infidel ear

Whose coffee smelled so sweet
In the night's descending breath

Alexander the emancipator of the serfs
Whose stooping shoulders are clay
In the moulding palms of grief
Refuses not to watch his children die

46

The oaths
The exhortations
The grinding of tumblers under the heel
Rinse out the ring of idle toasts

His eye persists as they bolt

    Grabbing their guts
    Wrapping their heads in their hands
    Pulping their mates
    Leaping the imploring hands of
    The stricken and the stranded
    Stamping the little father from their hearts
    Flinging away his blessing with the cartridge
    Pouch

He will not see death in such abundance
Or pain in such garlands again

Distantly
His own disintegration waits on him
The centrifugence of imperial flesh
The rushing to the corners of time of digit and wrist

6

The bed of the emperor rests its feet in earth
The cot of the next-to-God
As if out of humility he sought
To breathe the peasant's persistence

His boots are polished in the yard
The sound of the brushes reaches his ear

He could kiss him on the mouth
He could summon the buffer of boots
Aproned and ashamed
And kiss his mouth for frailty

But lies imperially still
Choosing the function of majesty
Over the immortal sign

In the hospital they stiffen
Or endure probes

Tomorrow he will bless survivors
And pin ribbons to the heroes' gowns

     to the strewers of limbs
     to the freely bleeding
     to the stomachless

The horror of knowing the power of his touch
Will light the dying eye

7

The Sultan's reverence for the telegraph
His debt to the infidel

The cables hang low as udders from timber poles
Bringing to the sublime ear

     massacres
     mutinies
     infringements of the truce
     violations of the frontier

The aromatic garden numbs the urgency
The pastel sail of the dhow
Appears and disappears
Between the shoulders of his ministers

He notices how short its passage is
In the time it takes to make a war

It can hardly have brought in its nets

He resorted to delegation always now
While distrusting everyone

And putting his name to the imperial despatch
Sees against the watermark his sprouting hairs

In the midst of argument the self incurs
The mutter of mortality
No deck of women can distract him from

They urge on him a progress to the disaffected provinces
By royal train from Bagdhad to Trebizond
But he is silent
Staring across the Straits

A cruiser made in South Shields unzips the placid pond

8

The peculiar innocence of the imperialist
His dismay at the phenomenon of revolt

The amazement of the liberator who discovered
The oppressed ate better than he did

The merchant cannot comprehend the quarrel
He bows with equal unctiousness to both sides

We tolerated their obscure customs

I dreamed whole villages would fall upon my neck

They wreck my store who smiled good morning once

The governor regrets the quality of troops
Sent by the Porte

Their tendency to
                send home valuables
                commandeer without chits
                pile rifles on the altars
                dislodge icons from monastery walls

Their incorrigible
                castrating of suspects
                violating of mothers
                burning the innocent in barns

Which brings unwelcome censure on an earnestly
Reforming government

Have we not lived here for five hundred years
The white-haired Turk marooned upon his mattress pleads

WHAT

FIVE HUNDRED

ONLY FIVE HUNDRED

I blind

I choke

I gouge

The sound of your muezzin
The smell of your women
The unextinguishable contempt that hangs in the eye

As for your shop

That will serve still
When Christian fingers work the till

9

The attention to detail
That characterized the razing of the village

The determination
The application
The single-mindedness

51

That attended this obscure act

The church particularly
The school particularly

These were not left with either brick
Or tile intact

A labour which might have
Raised monuments
Spanned rivers
Cultivated swamps

And the whole left so uniformly flat
As if the officers had gone about with rules
Surveying

Not that this took them many hours
Rather ecstasy made short work of it

We remark how pleasure can mock time
And muscles in a passion rarely ache

And so this handful smashed the shell
Quicker than Carthage fell under the rake
And marched off singing

Not lewd
Not drunk

But in a fellowship
As if it was bread they'd broken

In wars of cultures it is never enough to be dead

The night contained more pleas than moths
The wounded apologize without attention
To consistency

The derisive cry of the ear chopper
The exultant maimer as he makes of the collapsed
Expression pulp

The enemy shall have no character
The knife threshes the throat
                the lips also
                the nose also
                impertinent distinctions
A turnip trimmed for the stall

And the woman of the Kurd says at the threshold

Her sex rising
Her sex conspiring
Her fertility breathing its will

Enter at all doors of me
If you can prove your kill

The heads of muzhiks bowl from his bags

In battle it is good that many die
The battle without casualties being

    The sight of idle orderlies
    The field unlittered with those
    Rags once capable of speech
    The sleeping drums of lint

A POSITIVE DISENCHANTMENT

So all makers of films who pan the harvest
All poets who harp on the pity
The photographers of cemeteries which have no edge

Collude in the mystery of death

    Its arbitrary selections
    Its magnificent oversights
    Its showing itself like the
    Flagrant exposer of his parts

I lived while they dropped in piles
I passed by where they all ended
I continued while they ceased
While they reached only halfway
I attained the finish

The discreet politics of the rug maker

His stoicism conducts the motion of the needle
His unlifted head sees no atrocity

The tide spreading before the gunners laps his fringes
The swollen carts
The bullocks mad in the shafts
Shells making avalanches of the tiles
Do not distract his fingers from the knots

The worst catastrophe is not to die
But to lose stock

The violation of the daughter
The son's enlistment
The sudden eruption of the wife

These will be worked between the threads
Encompassed in the margins or the lozenge
The pattern's silent testimony to the weaver's wrath

The worst catastrophe is not to die
But to lose stock

He notices the uncommon scarlet of the sluice
And dyes a snatch of wool

Allah the provider
The colourer of the cloth

Some of the prisoners were beheaded

Those whose heads outlasted temper

Played cards with their captors

But always contriving to lose

*

The heads were stacked into a pyramid

The eyes staring outwards

Their collective gaze an uncomprehending basilisk

*

During the night the heads were heard

A cacophony of ill-will

So the camp was moved

Jackals stood still

Charmed by the tent-pegs' petulant patter

Those who exulted

And those who were only soldierlike

Those who cut the throats of the hurt

And the offerers of water bottles

And those who slit some throats

But rinsed the dust from others

Came to a common liquid in a winter march

It snowed and their uniforms were poorly made
It froze and there was no firewood
For reasons of religion they could not swallow pork

The wealth of army contractors
The deforestation of earlier campaigns
The Christian disdain of the goat

And the doctor in the fur pelisse

(The doctor must be warmer than his patients
If there is a single biscuit he must eat
Or a single cup of water he must drink)

Cut frostbite swiftly as the fishmonger beheads

His surgical knives
His mahogany instrument case
Exemplary products of industrial states

By the summer nothing showed among the wheats
The skulls were flung to the boundary
And the long bones pitched into stooks

15

Siege

The rat's bewilderment at sudden popularity

The consumption of the zoo

The moral recklessness of polite women

The birth of new humour

The passions of extremity which render subsequent
Existence pale

Breach

The frenzy of the exterior upon the interior

The spilling of the larder and the library

The punishment of the animate and the inanimate

As if delay made forfeit charity

The poet's horror at the fallibility of words

Troy's bleeding monuments

Massada's intoxicating leaps

Syracuse's innovative deaths

Acre's carpet of disfigured women

Wexford's mounds of the unchosen

Vienna's woods of castration

Lucknow's pond of fragments

Sebastopol's blinded dandies

Plevna's wails among the nightingales

Port Arthur's pulping of peasantries

Przemysl's pastrycooks burned on barbed wire

Kut's boiling clerks

Barcelona's shoving in shelters

Leningrad's sledging to funerals

Stalingrad's death on the assembly line

Berlin's flak of little boys

Dien Bien Phu's distance from Paris

Beirut's surgical cinemas

No surrender

Fight to the finish

The last drop of our

From under the ruins the cry will

Breathe

Defiance

Unto

The

Very

Unbending

Unyielding we

Un

Un

Un

And the women of his enemies in starched and pleated skirts
Pressed flowers on him

And the children of his victims in cornucopic hats
Draped garlands on his

Even the mothers of the slain and nurses of the amputees
Called him

Lion
Bull
Tiger

Praising his eyes
His porcine gaze is variously described as

Slate
Steel
Iron

HE GAVE NO QUARTER NOR EXPECTED NONE

We walk under siege
We besiege one another

The eye of the besieged in the queue
His sudden sally of abuse

HE YIELDED NOT AN INCH OF DIGNITY

The abandoned woman looks out from redoubts of contempt
The abandoned man reduces his ration again
The exhausted couple scour the horizon for relief

HERE I STAND AND HERE I

Out of Rodosto through the Straits
The captain of the dirty barquentine
Watches the palace of the Sultan pass
The terminus of slack telegraphs
And immaculate petitions
Under the deck a cargo of Christian
Vertebrae and Islamic ribs
The caliph does not lift his head
To watch his army pass
How could he guess the restless itinerary
Of the combattants?

The bones protest their exile in the swell
And in the Channel the cargo shifts
As if by numbers
Only guano from Cape Horn yields
Nitrates of such density
A bedroom in St Petersburg saw the baring
Of these imperfect teeth
And this wrist was cherished in Aleppo
The armies leech away in Wiltshire drains
And Cornish mists
God understands all this and Allah
Both provide
The cycle of indifference
The skeletal anabasis

The possibility hate is intrinsic
The possibility hate waits to be born with every birth
The possibility it sits in the same mouth as grief
And floods the lip with pity's pouring
Rising like mercury through the phial
Flashing like the casement catching sun
It succulence lending life to the tongue

Explain its durability among so much civility
    its persistence in the blizzard of understanding
    its howl amidst welfare
    its boldness in guilt

And how it thrives in innocent lives
Like the rat carrying its unwieldy gut along the
Grave channel

I Repeat Myself

Objectively it must be said
You have aged alarmingly
And what were only the
Suggestions of experience
Are dug in deep as history
Let us kiss therefore
Time is so much shorter
Than we thought

*

How I should like to see your breast
And always did
How I liked to see it unslung
How it affirmed
The obvious powers such as gravity
                          such as maternity
But the less obvious also such as pity
                          even aridity
                          even antiquity

*

You were my lover
And now fear I will ask again

And seeing you
I expect inevitably to ask again

As I also expect you inevitably
To look conciliatory thereby

Laying it to rest again

This at Least

Landscape being all reproduction now
Some usurpation of that afternoon
Inevitable
Some sense we played the parts
Demanded by the view

Let others note the scent of grasses
I refuse

I know a poet could capture the
Fractious tone of the timber saw
Crossed with the moves of the bee

Let him

And your brown belly reluctantly
Yet desperately exposed
Is counterfeited on every little screen

But you at least
Kept desire in a shape so vehemently secret
I defy whole armies of copiers
To enter in

Lend the Poor an Enemy

Lend the poor an enemy to feel their lives
Were not blindly blighted
And give the rich the gift of fear
Or they will never treasure what they accumulate

Look
I own nothing but my thought
Says the wise man
And in order not to stimulate
The anger of others
I walk in this filthy overcoat
Mumbling
Muttering
Hissing
I pretend to be mad
And perhaps
I have become so now

We Are Losing, So ...
(For Paul Freeman)

Because we are losing I wish to apologize
For what I would not have apologized for
Under any other circumstances

Because we are losing I have begun to notice
What I noticed before but only in the way
You glimpse a landscape
Routinely

So I ask for your forgiveness
I ask for magnanimity which is becoming in a winner
But not inevitable in a winner
I ask you to be what I could not myself be
When I was winning

And it will be easy for you
Because ironically the sufferers are quickest
To learn charity
Oddly enough the victim is more charitable
Than the criminal
Oddly
More
Charitable

In this way a new start can be made
The slate can be wiped clean
The house rebuilt
The garden planted all over again

And I will look you in the eyes without shame
Because my shame will mar our future
It is imperative I look you in the eyes without shame

And your look perhaps might be
And I suggest this cautiously
A little humble
Humbler even than before

Your superiority you see
Even though you try to expunge it
In the interests of equality
I inevitably will feel
Compensate me therefore
Say if you disagree

I am thinking of our future
In which all cruelty must be forgotten
As I will try to forget your cringing
Before the police dog's jaws
My feelings are no less delicate than yours
Perhaps more so
Guilt being so warping of the soul
How could you know
Who have only anger
Very clean thing
Very swift thing
Burns and quickly turns to ash
Whereas shame is in the marrow

So you will perhaps to aid me
Not complain if I remain offhand
Keeping some of the old distance
Some of the old arrogance
Ard the old blindness

And seeing me give you cold stares
Bring yourself to simply say
He was of the former dispensation
And his poor civility is pain

And should I curse you out of habit
Smile
Is that too much to ask
Smile
This has the flavour of impertinence
But I am thinking of the future

Arguably
And tell me if I go too far
You also might address me sir
You might say to your children
Call that man sir it pleases him
Adding
I would not be called sir for all the world

I believed in something untrue
Or more precisely
Sensing it to be untrue did not demur
Conscience did nothing
Only History
It is right I should be consigned thus

Absurd

We are losing
Or none of this could have occurred
To me

The Dance of Two Coolies

The idle peasant
Seeing the approach of strangers
Fled to the mountain
Throwing aside his rake

The energetic peasant
Sensing the prospect of advancement
Ran to greet them
Throwing aside his rake
Advertizing his health
Revealing his teeth
Submitting to examination for
Hernia
Piles
Malformation of the feet

Seeing the settling of the dust
The idle returned to his plot
Enduring the ridicule of
Abandoned wives
(He would sleep with them in time)
Relieved landlords
(These contracts rid him of the discontents)
Impeccable priests
(Of the opinion God helps the brave)
And living a poor life under a tree

The energetic was marched to a port
Behind two thousand others

Equally energetic
Equally ashamed of poverty
Equally perfect in health
And signed the indenture with his cross
The company providing

One passage to Peru
One pair of linen drawers
One mattress
One bowl
One space on a barrackroom floor

And a ship to China at the end of seven years
When unspent earnings would accumulate as high
As stars in the Antarctic night
Stars he glimpsed from underneath four decks
In sweltering pens of unplugged muscle

Some died
And this the energetic viewed without discouragement
Death being only

Old Death
Him again
Old him
Who must have boarded at Tienstin

Only the flinging of the corpses off the stern
Injured his sense of ritual

The idle all this time ate little
Was taxed twice over
Was splashed by the wheels
Of the whore's dogcart

And beaten first by the bandits
Second by the police
A routine and predictable life

They disembarked the energetic on a rock
Unwatered
Unvegetated
Dazzling white
Which when he set his foot on it
Was found to be
(The disbelief)
Was positively
(They giggled philosophically)
Entirely
SHIT
Shit Isles
Shit's imperium
The apotheosis of the cloaca
Whose dessication they would breathe
Whose paste in rain they skidded on
Whose makers squealed in flocks
Not only all the day
But all the night in harvesting
The anchovy

Seven years of the birds
And the bell of the soldiers' rifle butts
Clanging the hours on the ribs
The coolies turned the world over
The shovel
The terrible orchestra of the shovel
Manuring Norfolk
           Livorno
           Brittany

As the idle lay under the rain an army passed
Some fell under their wheels
Some were decapitated
Landlords usurped each other
The money changed its colour
And he regretted his idleness profoundly
He wept to recollect the chance he
                    the offer they
And cursing his character his ancestor
He kicked the mongrel whose howl sailed away
Like a kite
Through the turbulent Pacific
And
        fell
            among
                freighters
                    wallowing
                        off
                            quays

Where the energetic
(Sole survivor of the dysentry)
Now less energetic
(They had shortened the ration)
Doomed to extinction
(No one had lasted seven years)
Manure himself
(They buried you in shit)
Regretted his energy profoundly
And wept to recollect the chance he
                    the offer they

Cursing his character his ancestor
He bit the guard dog whose howl sailed away

A storm of sticks
A barrage of boots
Another one dead
And no bonus to pay

The coolies turned the world over
The shovel
The terrible orchestra of the shovel

When We Burned the Scientist

We burned him in a fire of kipper boxes
In the alley by the cinema
We tied him to a drainpipe and sang

The innumerate

He suffered for nearly an hour
And still the buses plied their routes
Some jeered and others left to post coupons

The illiterate

He had perfected the theory of expansion
In the superheated vessel
But a workman had spilled his tea on a switch

The dissolute

And the crowd had trapped him as he left
The inquiry into the deaths
We refused him permission to speak

The intolerant

His predecessors slew the dragon of plague
Look at your child if you require his defence
The boy's health the girl's intelligence

The innoculated

Human error is all that stands between
The shivering widow and cheap heat
To which we bawled
We are human and we err

The incorrigible

At Least It Was Evil

Have you not studied the plagues of political death
At least they were hated

At least they were victims of somebody's whim
There was consolation in it

The loathing of the persecutor as he slams the door
The casual indifference of the switch

There is evil at least in being murdered
If only for the shape of your head

Instead

We are dying now for curiosity
We are dying for the decent human habit
Of interfering with things

Educate that out of the psyche

You would have to create children who did not
When looking at the caterpillar
Study its avoidance of the fingernail

Who looked in the pond and only looked

Who watched without changing
Who knew without altering
Who willingly suffered a curable death

We are dying so innocently now

No machine guns

How calm it is outside the laboratories

A Rebuke to the Socialist David Blunkett
For Quitting the Play 'A Passion in Six Days'

Joseph Stalin left silently the opera
Lady Macbeth of Mtsensk
Thereby consigning the work to obscurity
From which it eventually emerged
Though possibly it might never have emerged
Because it lies in the power of dictators
To expunge even a man's kindness
From the memory of his friends

Whereupon the composer changed his tune

The play did not appeal to you
Though you know socialism creaks with pain
As well as I though probably I describe it better
Certainly I brought poetry to it
I showed men and women sometimes chanting
And sometimes making love for different reasons
Honest and dishonest reasons but this also
Is the proper field for socialism
It is difficult to talk of socialism
It is also difficult to talk of love

The actors dared and you did not

Rare Visitor

Here we sit
My brother and I
Grey at the hair roots
Over the halfway mark and him ill
And still he finds conversation difficult
While I trail questions like a lover who has
Become intoxicated with impatience and therefore
Chances the terrible and the trivial with equal rashness

*

My children
Rush to their uncle
Unlocking and kicking back
The doors of their hearts and their
Arms are wild semaphores for the stranger
Who must be good or how could he be born of the
Same mother he requires nothing he yields nothing and
So on his pale mask they inscribe the necessary mysteries

Factory Store

Here my grandmother sat drumming
The hours out of her life
And here my father was beaten
Here I stroked the black mongrel
A bored boy
Here my uncle's brilliant airforce boots
Stood unyielding

And the forklift truck bounds
A frisky animal
Over the spirit of the garden

Deeper
Deeper
You persistent improvers of the terrain

A First Lullaby for the Impatient

Sit down
We have this yard and the sun is not set
It burns without temper
Do sit
We have this bench which the worm has attacked
But not maliciously
Take the weight off your feet
The moss is abundant where there is shadow
It has its mission also
Do you sense the extinction of kindness
Asking me to approve your acts?
I will approve your acts
But now let us briefly suspend
The roar of impulse and of calculation
Hold my hands
The song of the neighbour never distracts
Nor the rattle of news
Nor the populace assenting
Endlessly assenting
This urge to laugh
This urge to clap
Man is in the pull of himself
As the gnats under the bough

Weave dependence into a trap
Certainly I will approve your acts
But sleep now
Lay your head on my shoulder
Your face is a blood soaked map
Etched with symbols of distance
And your hand is tight as a knife
Even when kissing

WILLIAM BARNES 1801-1886

By Dr. BERNARD JONES

Original Water Colour Sketch of William Barnes in old age. From Sketch Book (1879-1890) of John Leslie, artist, in the Dorset County Museum.

Of the many-mindedness of William Barnes many books could be made, for his life was of victorian breadth. To the Dorset County Museum he stands as one of the founding fathers, for when in 1845 the railway companies planned to lay their tracks into Dorchester Barnes was one of the people who, fearing that ancient earthworks might be broken up and archaeological remains wantonly thrown aside, met to protest. Out of this meeting grew the museum, and Barnes and the Rev. C. W. Bingham were elected its first secretaries in 1846. The museum collections were first housed in part of Judge Jeffreys' Lodgings in H gh West Street, were later moved to part of a house in what is now Trinity Street, and in 1883 were set out in the present building, which is the work of G. R. Crickmay, who took over the business of Thomas Hardy's first architecture master, John Hicks, and for whom Hardy worked for a short time. The museum today, then, is only over the road from its first home.

Although Barnes often called Dorchester 'the home of my heart', he was not a Dorchester man. All his youth he spent in the stretches of Blackmore Vale around Sturminster Newton. He worked as a solicitor's clerk in Dorchester from 1818 to 1823, but then he again went up into the Blackmore country for another twelve years to keep his school at Mere in Wiltshire. However, he moved his school to Dorchester in 1835, and when he gave it up in 1862 on becoming Rector of Came his rectory was no more than two miles from the town.

Barnes's schooling ended at the age of thirteen or fourteen years when he became a solicitor's engrossing clerk, but with the help of friendly neighbours he mastered steadily wide fields of learning. At the time of the founding of the museum he knew many languages and was a keen student of the sciences, history, archaeology and philology. His name had been on the boards at St. John's College, Cambridge, since 1838 and he was to become a B.D. in 1850. He had written many text books and had long been a busy writer and reviewer for the magazines. Moreover, his *Poems of Rural Life in the Dorset Dialect* had been widely praised since it came out in 1844, and he had ready another volume of poems in what he called 'national English', that is, standard English. In the book of dialect poems there was an important essay on Dorset speech and the first of his glossaries of Dorset words. The easy skill of the poet could be felt in the first verses of the first poem of the collection:

When wintry weather's all a-done,
An' brooks do sparkle in the zun,
An' naïsy-builden rooks do vlee
Wi' sticks toward their elem tree;
When birds do zing, an' we can zee
 Upon the boughs the buds o' spring,—
Then I'm as happy as a king,
 A-vield wi' health an' zunsheen.

But in 1846 the tide turned against him. The master of Hardye's, the Dorchester Grammar School, retired and, in his own eyes at least, Barnes was led to understand that he would be offered the place. The feoffees, or governors, of the school, however, behaved so awkwardly that they seemed only to wish to keep Barnes out and to make their own rules to this end. Barnes felt the wound deeply, and all the more so when one of his friends told him that it was undignified to complain. The feoffees may have been thrown into disarray at the thought of making headmaster a man who not only had not been through a grammar school, but one who also wrote dialect poetry, and therefore, perhaps, against the judgments of poets and the learned, they decided that he could not be put in charge of the sons of honest tradesmen and clergymen. Besides, he wore strange hats and something that looked like a mixture of cassock and dressing gown.

Barnes had already left his first Dorchester house in Durngate Street for one next to Napper's Mite in South Street. His answer to the feoffees was to buy a still bigger house on the other, the west, side of South Street. But although things seemed well for a time, he had lost friends. He grew more and more keen on his studies. In 1852 his wife died and he was left with six children to look after. The school slowly ran down and by 1862 was almost at a standstill. Even then his pupil Hooper Tolbort, a friend of Hardy, headed the Indian Civil Service examination list, and in these last years he had a number of boys whose names were not to be wholly forgotten: Frederick Treves, who became a surgeon; Joseph Clarke. who became an artist; Octavius Pickard-Cambridge, who became a naturalist; Benjamin Fossett Lock, who became a judge; Walter Lock, who became Warden of Keble College, Oxford; and J. J. Foster, who became an art historian.

Barnes bore no ill will to the master of Hardye's, and their boys were soon out on the cricket field. And when he had finished teaching Barnes examined the Hardye's School boys. But the wilfulness of the feoffees was a great shock to him and probably turned his mind away from teaching. He became curate of Whitcombe in 1847 and, although he gave up the curacy just before his wife's death, he looked more and more to the Church as his true calling. In 1862, when he had been in need of £30 of the royal bounty and when his friends had at last got him a civil list pension, he had the great happiness of being presented to the living of Winterborne Came with Whitcombe. From Came Rectory by the Wareham road he looked after his parishioners for the next twenty-four years. There he was called on by Tennyson, Allingham, Patmore, Palgrave, Quiller-Couch, Gosse, the Chevalier de Chatelain, Prince Lucien Buonaparte and, of course, Hardy, who made a poem of the flash of sunlight on the brass of his old friend's coffin. Hicks the architect had his office next door to Barnes's last school, and the home at Max Gate, which Hardy built a few years before Barnes's death, looked over to the rectory.

Until well into the nineteen-fifties many people whose childhood was spent in Dorchester could recall Barnes as he is shewn in Roscoe Mullins's statue in St. Peter's Churchyard, or in the same sculptor's statuette in the museum. He would walk into town from Came in silver buckled shoes and staff in hand, and make his way along the middle of South Street past the select villas where he had once taught, and which have long given way to the boring monotony of tasteless shop fronts. After setting his watch by the town clock he would go about his business, perhaps seeing his tradespeople, or calling on his printer or the newspaper office, perhaps stepping over to the mueseum to check his latest archaeological finds or to read one of his historical or archaeological papers to the Dorset Field Club, of which he was a founder member. Thirty or forty years earlier he would have been a lively stepping body of middle height, with twinkling light blue eyes and shewing, until he fell for the late victorian fashion of the wild beard, a soft pale-skinned face. At times he could be tiresomely victorian indeed, as when he wrote at length on the dry earth closet system of his friend the Rev. Henry Moule of Fordington. Barnes seems to have thought it better than the water closet not because he thought it more sanitary, or more useful where there was no piped water, but because he believed it was more in keeping with the mind of the Almighty. On the other hand, he was always full of fun and had a neat kind of wit. After hearing a well known archaeologist say in Dorchester that the further he went west, the more sure he was that the wise men came from the east, Barnes answered that of course they did, and they had never gone back.

Barnes would have earned the kindly thoughts of Dorset folk if he had done no more than write the dissertation and glossary of 1844. He revised these in 1847, for the Philological Society in 1863, and again just before his death. He knew that in his own lifetime the dialect speech he had heard in Blackmore Vale had waned and he did all he could to leave behind a true record of its shape. His other writings on speech, such as *A Philological Grammar* (1854), *Tiw* (1862), which he named after the race god of the Teutons, and *An Outline of English Speech-craft* (1878) could not be grounded on first hand knowledge as were his books on Dorset speech. They are best thought of as early reachings out towards a science of comparative philology, for Barnes was an old man before the Philological Society and the *New English Dictionary* got under way. Even so, much can be learnt from these books. In the last of them, and in *An Outline of Rede-craft* (1879), Barnes gave Saxon names for the classical terms of grammar and logic. Here again much can be learnt from him, although the books have left no mark on the study of these subjects.

The knowledge Barnes won from speech lore gave much interest to his two history books, *Notes on Ancient Britain and the Britons* (1858), and *Early England and the Saxon-English* (1869), for he was able to give not only neat sketches of the two literatures but also to use etymology to cast light on history itself. Lest it should seem that Barnes always wrote of the past his *Views of Labour and Gold* (1859) should not be overlooked. It is a closely wrought weighing up of English society and economics at the height of the victorian age, and the picture it gives could hardly have been more gloomy.

But although Barnes's work for Dorset speech and for the museum might have been enough to make him simply a Dorset worthy, the rest of the world would have forgotten him if he had not been one of the most delightful poets of his time. Between 1819 and 1886 Barnes wrote over eight hundred poems. The early ones are rather weak and there are some dull religious verses, but from the time of the book of 1844, which represents some ten years' composition, until his death, the level is very high. One of the best poems was set to music by Ralph Vaughan Williams at the beginning of this century and it is now so well known that it has been announced on the wireless as a folk song:

'Ithin the woodlands, flow'ry gleäded,
By the woak tree's mossy moot,
The sheenen grass-bleädes, timber-sheäded,
Now do quiver under voot;
An' birds do whissle over head,
An' water's bubblen in its bed,
An' there vor me the apple tree
Do leän down low in Linden Lea.

When leaves that leätely wer a-springen
Now do feäde 'ithin the copse,
An' painted birds do hush their zingen
Up upon the timber's tops;
An' brown-leav'd fruit's a-turnen red,
In cloudless zunsheen, over head,
Wi' fruit vor me, the apple tree
Do leän down low in Linden Lea.

Let over vo'k meäke money vaster
In the aïr o' dark-room'd towns,
I don't dread a peevish meäster;
Though noo man do heed my frowns,
I be free to goo abrode,
Or teäke ageän my hwomeward road
To where, vor me, the apple tree
Do leän down low in Linden Lea.

Most of Barnes's best qualities can be found in this poem. The meaning is clear, the pictures are clear, and the music of the words is wholly fitting. The refrain, or burden as Barnes would have called it, follows the consonantal pattern of Welsh poetry, and shews, therefore, how useful philology could be to the poet. The only word not widely known is *moot*, which means the roots and remains of a felled tree.

MY ORCHA'D IN LINDEN LEA is one of the poems of Barnes's second dialect collection of 1859. Another collection followed in 1862. Much of his poetry is in plain English, however. Apart from two early booklets, Barnes published collections of English poems in 1846, 1868 and 1870, and many poems were uncollected when he died. The first collection of all Barnes's poems was published only in 1962, by the Centaur Press.

The English no less than the dialect poems have the ring of the poet's own voice:

THE HILL-SHADE

At such a time, of year and day,
  In ages gone, that steep hill-brow
Cast down an evening shade, that lay
  In shape the same as lies there now.
Though then no shadows wheel'd around
The things that now are on the ground.

The hill's high shape may long outstand
  The house, of slowly-wasting stone;
The house may longer shade the land
  Than man's on-gliding shade is shown;
The man himself may longer stay
Than stands the summer's rick of hay.

The trees that rise, with boughs o'er boughs,
  To me for trees long-fall'n may pass;
And I could take those red-hair'd cows
  For those that pull'd my first-known grass;
Our flow'rs seem yet on ground and spray,
But oh, our people; where are they?

There has been argument about whether the English or the dialect poems are best, but the argument is not worthwhile. The dialect poems are easier to read than Burns's well-known Scots poems and the English poems far better than those who only want a country poet to sound quaint allow. The truth is that few of the poets of Barnes's day stand above him. This particular Dorset worthy, indeed, is far too important to be locked away in his own county, for his poetry offers a rich store of delight to anyone who loves the music of English speech and pictures of country ways.

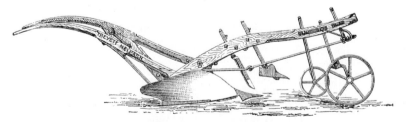

The tail-piece is from an original design by William Barnes.

SOME DORSET FOLKLORE

By WILLIAM BARNES

WEST COUNTRY FOLKLORE SERIES

INTRODUCTION TO THE SERIES
By Theo Brown, General Editor.

There is an increasing interest in folklore at the present time. Yet there are few subjects so abused and devalued, and there seems to be a real need for reliable information and some indication of its proper place in modern knowledge, and its relationship to life. This implies firstly, accurate description, secondly a sane, scholarly evaluation, thirdly an awareness of history and locality, and a respect for the strange ideas held by other people, whether or not they hold good in our civilisation; and I would add, fourthly, a sense of poetry, which sometimes gives a clue to that irrational mythology of the mind, that obtains—whether we like it or not—in every stage of human development, all over the world and in every period.

In this series we hope to deal with various problems of this kind as they are found in the west country. The authors are all well-known authorities on the subjects they discuss. Folklorists, almost by definition, are individualists, so their views will be diverse, and this freedom of movement within the series should lead to a very lively and useful collection of monographs.

General Editor :
Miss THEO BROWN.

Assistant Editor :
J. STEVENS COX, Esq., F.S.A.

Honorary Advisors :
H. S. L. DEWAR, Esq.
H. F. V. JOHNSTONE, Esq.
G. STEVENS COX, Esq.

Harvest-Home, 1838.
From Hone's Every-Day Book, 1838.

WEST COUNTRY FOLKLORE No. 3

General Editor: THEO BROWN.

Some Dorset Folklore

By WILLIAM BARNES

The Toucan Press, Mount Durand, St. Peter Port, C.I.. via Britain.

1969

INTRODUCTION

By Theo Brown

The Rev. William Barnes, B.D. (1800-1886) was primarily a philologist, but he is best loved as a 'rustic' poet in the Dorset dialect. He was born at Rushay, near Pentridge. He lived subsequently at Sturminster Newton, Dorchester, Mere in Wiltshire, Whitcombe near Dorchester, and Winterbourne Came. He wrote very little specifically on folklore. Just before his death he wrote the excellent 'Fore-say' for J.S. Udal's *Dorsetshire Folk-Lore* (1922) in which he suggested two 'levels' of folklore, one of childhood and one of the full-grown. As a young man he had contributed a number of interesting notes to Hone's *Year Book* (1832) which we are extracting.

SOME DORSET FOLKLORE

By WILLIAM BARNES.

(From Hone's Year Book, 1832)

Harvest Home—Hay making—Matrimonial Oracles—Midsummer Eve Peace in 1814—Country Fairs—Perambulations.

Harvest Home, formerly celebrated with great mirth, but now a declining usage, was a feast given by the farmer at the end of harvest, or when his hay and corn were got in. " *O fortunatos nimium, sua sibona nôrint, agricolas,*" says Virgil; how happy, if they knew their bliss, are farmers! yet this like all other happiness, has its alloy. The farmer's seed is scattered upon the surface of his field, where it receives the attentions of a nurse, and yet sometimes perishes with his hopes; he has anxieties for the firstlings of his flock, exposed to the storms of March, and many die from inclemency; bad weather, unhealthy and thin crops, fluctuations of market, loss of cattle, inroads of thieves, and unfaithfulness of servants, often disturb the farmer's peace; and, if we have not a just confidence in the wisdom and goodness of God, he is an unhappy and ill-tempered man. Some years ago the "Harvest-home" in my native county, Dorset, was kept up with good old English hospitality. When the last load was ricked, the laborers, male and female, the swarthy reaper, and the sun-burnt hay-maker, the saucy boy who had not seen twelve summers, and the staff horny handed old mower who had borne the toil of fifty, all made a happy group, and went with singing the loud-laughing to the "harvest-home supper" at the farm-house, where they were expected by the good mistress, dressed in a quilted petticoat and a linsey-wolsey apron, with shoes fastened by large silver buckles which extended over her foot like a pack-saddle on a donkey.(1) The dame and her husband welcomed them to a supper

---

(1) William Barnes wore this type of shoe until the end of his life.

5

of good wholesome food, a round of beef, and a piece of bacon, and perhaps the host and hostess had gone so far as to kill a fowl or two, or stick a turkey, which had fattened in the wheat yard. This plain English fare was eaten from wooden trenchers, by the side of which were put little cups of horn filled with beer or cider. When the cloth was removed, one of the men, putting forth his large hand like the gauntlet of an armed knight, would grasp his horn of beer, and standing on a pair of legs which had long out-grown the largest holes of the village stocks, and with a voice which, if he had not been speaking a dialect of the English language, you might have thought came from the deep-seated lungs of a lion, he would propose the health of the farmer in the following lines:—

> Here's a health unto miaster
> The founder of the feast,
> And I hope to God wi' all my heart
> His soul in heaven mid rest;
> That every thing mid prosper
> That ever he tiak in hand,
> Vor we be all his servants,
> And all at his command.

After this would follow a course of jokes, anecdotes, and songs, in some of which the whole company joined, without attention to the technicalities of counter-point, bass, tenor, and treble, common chords and major thirds; but each singing the air and pitching in at the key that best fitted his voice, making a medley of big and little sounds, like the lowings of oxen and the low bleatings of old ewes, mixed up with the shrill pipings of the lambs at a fair. The conversation commonly turned on the incidents of the summer: how the hay-makers overtook the mowers, or how the rain kept the labor back, how they all crept in a heap under the waggon in a thunderstorm; how nearly some of them were crushed under the load that was upset; who was the best mower or reaper in the village; which field yielded the best crop; and which stack was most likely to heat.

Hay-making is one of the most pleasing occupations of an English summer. The bright green of the smooth mown fields, bordered by "hedge-row elms," the sweet smell of the new hay, the bustle and merry songs of the busy hay-makers, and the waving uncut crops, are to the peaceful mind of a thinking observer really charming. In the hay-field the master distributes his men with the same attention to their abilities as the manager of a theatre casts the characters of a play among his performers. The younger and less experienced are set to rake the hay up unto ridges, called in Dorset "wales," or to put it up into cocks; some of that numerous class of laborers who have more strength than wit are sent to pitch or unload; the next "grade," as brother Jonathan says, is that of the loader, who must be a man of some little talent, to build the load upright, and make it firm by properly putting in the binding masses at the corners but the highest rank is that of the rick or stack-maker, who, besides having a proper knowledge of the mathematical lines under which hay-stacks are commonly comprehended, must be a man of activity and strength. The ground shape of the rick is either

6

a circle or a parallelogram, which is to be correctly kept; the rick must be upright, rounded out in the middle, and then go off into a cone or pyramid; and the rick-maker must so fix its size that it may take all the hay intended to be put into it, without spoiling its shape and without waste or want! or, in the expression of the hay-makers, "with none to leave and none to lack."

Matrimonial Oracles, and Midsummer Eve.—When we think on the consequences of a woman's marriage—that she may be dragged into a long train of evils, and her heart be broken by a profligate or indolent partner—or be led smiling in well-being through life, by a man of virtue and good sense:—when we see a happy girl, and imagine what may be her fate—subjected to the unkind treatment and coarse language of a boor, or have her mind soothed and exalted by the conversation of a well-acting and right-thinking Christian man;—whether, like another Penelope, she is to regret the absence of a husband wandering in other lands, or navigating the stormy deep; to be united to a home-dwelling partner, and make with him a pair as inseparable as the two staves of a piece of music for the pianoforte, and as like a sentiment as the two texts of a biglot Bible;—whether she is to inhabit the "flaunting town," or to live in the quiet farms and fields;—when we think and reflect that her destiny depends upon him whom she chooses for better or for worse, we cannot be surprised that young females hanker to know what sort of men the fates have given them for husbands, even at an early age.

In my childhood, a time when—as Pertrarch says of old age— little lovers may be allowed

"Sedersi insieme, e dir che lor incontra,"

to sit together, and say whatever comes into their heads; when the pretty name of Flora or Fanny was not a whit more charming to me than Tom or Jack; and when a pound of marbles, with half a score of shouting boy-playmates, were as pleasing as a dance with a party of smiling, rosy girls; I recollect some of my female friends, while gathering flowers in a meadow, would stop, and, plucking a large daisy, pull off the petals one by one, repeating at the same time the words

"Rich man, poor man, farmer, ploughman, thief;"

fancying, very seriously, that the one which came to be named at plucking the last petal would be her husband. Another way of knowing the future husband (inferior only to the dark words of that high priestess of the oracles of Hymen, the cunning gypsey), is, to pluck an even ash-leaf, and, putting it into the hand, to say,

"The even ash-leaf in my hand,
"The first I meet shall be my man."

Then, putting it into the glove, to say,
"The even ash-leaf in my glove,
"The first I meet shall be my love."

And, lastly, into the bosom, saying,
"The even ash-leaf in my bosom,
"The first I meet shall be my husband."

7

Soon after which the future husband will make his appearance, and the lass may observe him as accurately as she will.

Midsummer Eve, however, is the great time with girls for discovering who shall be their husbands; why it is so, more than any other, I cannot tell, unless, indeed, the sign Gemini, which the sun then leaves, is symbolical of the wedding union; but, however that may be, a maiden will walk through the garden at midsummer, with a rake on her left shoulder, and throw hemp-seed over her right, saying, at the same time,

"Hemp-seed I set, hemp-seed I sow,
"The man that is my true-love come after me and mow."

It is said by many who have never tried it, and some who have, without effect, that the future husband of the hemp-sowing girl will appear behind her with a scythe, and look as substantial as a brass image of Saturn on an old time-piece. Or if, at going to bed, she put her shoes at right angles with each other, in the shape of a T, and say,

"Hoping this night my true love to see,
"I place my shoes in the form of a T."

they say she will be sure to see her husband in a dream, and perhaps in reality, by her bed-side. Besides this, there is another method of divination. A girl, on going to bed, is to write the alphabet on small pieces of paper, and put them into a bason of water with the letters downward; and it is said that in the morning she will find the first letter of her husband's name turned up, and the others as they were left.

The celebration of Peace, in August, 1814, took place when I was a boy, old enough to enjoy the merry doings at my native village, and to remember them till now. The respectable inhabitants subscribed largely to treat the poor with a public dinner of beef and pudding, and strong beer. Their festival was held in a field by the river side, where several hundreds of people, young and old, sat down at two long lines of tables. Their hearing was gratified by the lively music of a band; and their taste and smell by the savour of a wholesome old English meal, at which they held their noses for an hour over the steam of boiled beef, or thrust them at intervals into the cool deepening vacuum of the beer jug. Their sight was afterwards indulged with spectacles of village merry-making; and their feelings by the twistings and twinings, and spirit-stirring hop, skip, and jump agitations of the dance : gallopades were not then invented, or two thousand people might have hopped along in a string, like a row of little mop-stem-riding boys on their wooden horses. Among the sports were *Jumping in sacks,* thus performed : —half a dozen men were put into as many sacks, which were tied round their necks, and gave them the shape of a row of blacking jars in a shop. In this state they were to hop a given distance for the mastery and, as they could not erect themselves into the natural perpendicular of the human body, when they fell down, there were what may have been called resurrection men, to help them up. There was *Grinning through horse-collars,* in which the winner is he who can thrust through a horse's collar the ugliest sample of a human face, either by showing the odd substitutes which nature might have stuck in his head for features, or else by ristorting them into something still more unlike, and uglier than natural features. Besides these there was *Running by young women,* a sport in which the victress received a white holland shift; not without having shown, however, by the high upflinging of her "light fantasic toe" in the race, that she could mark her initials, and, at least No. 2, upon it. *Running for the pig* with the greased tail was a famous general chase, in which the individual who caught the pig by the tail became its lawful owner—when, after many long strides and hard strainings, many a breathless wight overtook the galloping porker, and grasped the slippery little member, *"Heu omnis effusus labor!"* it slipped through the fingers, and the trotters carried off the head, hams, and sides, at full speed, till a dexterous victor made them his own. An effigy of Buonaparte was also carried about: this the good people first hung, then shot, and lastly burnt; thus securing the arch enemy of England by various deaths, as, in a suit at law, the plaintiff secureth the defendant by the various counts in the declaration.

The Fair Day is to the milk-maids and striplings of some villages one of the brightest in their calendar. As the time approaches to it, their joy rises, like the mercury in a barometer at the comnig of fine weather. The children lessen their outlay for toys and sweetmeats, and hoard the saved pence; and the trite observation on meeting friends, that "it is fine weather," gives place to the earnest question, "Be gwain to fa-yer o' Monday?" Some time ago, on a fine day in September, I went to a famous fair, held at the foot of one of the green hills of Dorset. When I first set out I walked along the still shady lanes alone, but, as I drew near the fair-place, I commingled with a stream of people, all tending to the same point. There were groups of white-gowned, red-faced lasses, led by their swains with bunches of flowers stuck in the button-holes of their long blue coats, and switching in one hand a tough ground-ash stick. I had not a fair mate myself, and could well listen to their observations. "How much money hast got vor fayer?" said a ruddy little boy to another, whom he had a little before overtaken. "Zix-pence," said the other, with a grin of satisfaction; thumping his hand on his pocket, and erecting his body into a posture of dignity he thought himself entitled to by his wealth. Alas! thought I, how true is it that our wants are only imaginary, and that riches and poverty are only relative terms! this boy is proud to go to fair with his six-pence, while many spend-thrifts think themselves stinted if they have not hundreds to squander in things as worthless as those that will be bought by him. With these thoughts in my mind, my attention was drawn to the rude, though well-meant, salutation of a Dorset swain, who, seeing a friend forward, crept softly behind him, and with the full force of an arm which had perhaps been long exercised in mowing, or swinging the flail, laid his stick athwart his back, upon which his acquaintance looked round, and received his assailant with a hearty shake of the hand. I was by this time in the fair, where the din of drums and horns at the shows, the loud invitation, "Walk up, walk up," of the showmen, the hum of voices, the squeaking of fiddles, and the creaking of rattles, made

9

altogether a medley of sounds which, supposing with Pope "all discord harmony not understood," would have been very pleasing to my ear, but for my ignorance of harmony. Seeing a merry-Andrew come out at one of the shows, I went up to listen to a few of his much-repeated, though still laugh-stirring jokes. He was surrounded by a crowd of starers, with their faces all worked up into grins, so exactly like his own that they seemed reflections of his own—like the faces you would see were you to twist your mouth to the expression of drolling laughter, and look into a multiplying glass. The dense crowd around the show was, however, suddenly scattered by a bull. He had escaped from the cattle-fair, to exhibit himself at full run among the standings, where he was received with chuckles and shouts by those who were out of his way, and with screams from women and children in his line of race: after a short peep at the humours of the fair, he was prevailed upon to retire, and leave the bipeds to their former fun. I withdrew with the coming on of the evening: as I would round the hill the noise of the fair died gradually away, and I reached my home in silence.

A Perambulation, or, as it might be more correctly called, a circumambulation, is the custom of going round the boundaries of a manor or parish, with witnesses, to determine and preserve recollection of its extent, and to see that no encroachments have been made upon it, and that the landmarks have not been taken away. It is a proceeding commonly regulated by the steward, who takes with him a few men and several boys who are required to particularly observe the boundary lines traced out, and thereby qualify themselves for witnesses, in the event of any dispute about the landmarks or extent of the manor, at a future day. In order that they may not forget the lines and marks of separation, they "take *pains*" at almost every turning. For instance, if the boundary be a stream, one of the boys is tossed into it; if a broad ditch, the boys are offered money to jump over it, in which they of course fail, and pitch into the mud, where they stick as firmly as if they had been rooted there for the season; if a hedge, a sapling is cut out of it, and used in afflicting that part of their bodies upon which they rest in the posture between standing and lying; if a wall, they are to have a race on the top of it, when, in trying to pass each other, they fall over on each side,—some descending, perhaps, into the still stygian waters of a ditch, and others thrusting the "human face divine" into a bed of nettles: if the boundary be a sunny bank, they sit down upon it, and get a treat of beer, and bread and cheese, and, perhaps, a glass of spirits. When these boys grow up to be men, if it happens that one of them should be asked if a particular stream were the boundary of the manor he had perambulated, he would be sure to say, in the manner of Sancho Panca, "Ees, that 'tis, I'm sure o't, by the same token that I were tossed into't, and paddled about there lik a water-rot, till I wor hafe dead." If he should be asked whether the aforesaid pleasant bank were a boundary,—"O, ees it be," he would say, "that's where we squat down, and tucked in a skinvull of vittles and drink." With regard to any boundary perambulated after that, he would most likely declare, "I won't be sartin; I got zo muddled up top o' the banks, that don' know where we ambulated arter that."

SINGLE-STICK AND CUDGELS

I do not observe that you notice the yearly village sports of Single-stick playing and Cudgelling, in your *Year-Book*.—You may know, perhaps, that the inhabitants of many of the villages in the western counties, not having a fair or other merry-making to collect a fun-seeking money-spending crowd, and being willing to have one day of mirth in the year, have some time in the summer what are called *feasts;* when they are generally visited by their friends, whom they treat with the old English fare of beef and plumb pudding, followed by the sports of single-stick playing, cudgelling, or wrestling: and sometimes by those delectable inventions of merry Comus, and mirthful spectacles of the village green, jumping in the sack, grinning through the horse-collar, or the running of blushing damsels for that indispensable article of female dress—the plain English name of which rhymes with a *frock*(1).

Single-stick playing is so called to distinguish it from cudgelling, in which two sticks are used: the single-stick player having the left hand tied down, and using only one stick both to defend himself and strike his antagonist. The object of each gamester in this play, as in cudgelling, is to guard himself, and to fetch blood from the other's head; whether by taking a little skin from his pericranium, drawing a stream from his nose, or knocking out a few of those early inventions for grinding—the teeth.

They are both *sanguine* in their hope of victory, and, as many other ambitious fighters have done, they both aim at the *crown*.

In cudgelling, as the name implies, the weapon is a stout cudgel; and the player defends himself with another having a large hemisphere of wicker-work upon it. This is called the *pot*, either from its likeness in shape to that kitchen article, or else in commemoration of some ancient warfare, when the " rude forefathers of the hamlet," being suddenly surrounded with their foes, sallied forth against them. armed with the *pot* and *ladle*.

Single-stick playing, and cudgelling, would be more useful to a man as an art of self-defence, if he were sure that his enemy would always use the same mode of fighting: but the worst of it is, if a Somersetshire single-stick player quarrel with a Devonshire wrestler, the latter, not thinking himself bound to crack the stickler's head by the rules of the game, will probobly run in and throw him off his legs, giving such a violent shock to his system that the only use he will be able to make of his stick will be that of hobbling home with it.

LENT-CROCKING.

In some of the villages of Dorsetshire and Wiltshire, the boys, at Shrovetide, still keep up a custom called *Lent-Crocking*, which

---

(1) Smock. A linen garment that was worn by women next to their bodies. In England, the smock was commonly given to girls as a prize in races from at least the early 18th c. and probably earlier. " See here this prize, this rich lac'd smock behold." (Somerville. *Hobbinol,* 1740.) Editor.

11

originated in the carnival of Roman Catholic times, and consists in going round in the evening to pelt the doors of the inhabitants with pieces of broken crockery.

In Dorsetshire, the boys sometimes go round in small parties; and the leader goes up and knocks at the door, leaving his followers behind him, armed with a good stock of potsherds—the collected relics of the washing-pans, jugs, dishes, and plates, that have become the victims of concussion in the unlucky hands of careless house-wives for the past year. When the door is opened, the hero, who is perhaps a farmer's boy, with a pair of black eyes sparkling under the tattered brim of his brown milking-hat covered with cow's hair and dirt like the inside of a black-bird's nest, hangs down his head, and, with one corner of his mouth turned up into an irrepressible smile, pronounces, in the dialect of his county, the following lines: composed for the occasion, perhaps, by some mendicant friar whose name might have been suppressed with the monasteries by Henry VIII.

> "I be come a shrovin,
> Vor a little pankiak,
> A bit o' bread o' your biakin.
> Or a little truckle cheese o' your own miakin,
> If you'll gi' me a little, I'll ax no moore,
> If you don't gi' me nothin, I'll rottle your door."

Sometimes he gets a piece of bread and cheese: and at some houses he is told to be gone, when he calls up his followers to send their missiles in a rattling broadside against the door.

In Wiltshire, the begging of pancake and bread and cheese is omitted; and the Lent-crockers pelt the doors as a matter of course.

The broken pots and dishes originally signified that, as Lent was begun, those cooking vessels were of no use, and were supposed to be broken; and the cessation of flesh-eating is understood in the begging for pancakes, and bread and cheese.

WEST COUNTRY FOLKLORE

1 The Giant of Cerne Abbas
   By H. S. L. Dewar, 1968   2/6 (0.30 c.)

2 Ghostly Gold and Goblin Tunes
   By Theo Brown and H. S. L. Dewar, 1969   2/6 (0.30 c.)

3 Some Dorset Folklore
   By William Barnes, 1969   2/6 (0.30 c.)

IN PREPARATION

King Arthur in the West Country.

West Country Charmers.

Brutus and Trojan.

Drake's Drum.

The Black Dog in the West Country.

The Devil's Footprints: The Great Devon Mystery of 1855.

White Horse Hill Figures.

If you would like to receive copies of these Monographs as they are issued, please send your name and address to the publisher: J. Stevens Cox, The Toucan Press, Mount Durand, St. Peter Port, Guernsey, via Britain, or place an order with your regular bookseller.

The Effect of Dancers on Poets

The dancers caused me to think
What future could there be for the word
They moved so fluently
The musicians caused me to wince
At the terrible fate of language
They thrilled so easily

In the costume of peasants the women
Offered themselves to the men
How brilliantly their tights flashed
From under the froth of lace
And the men pretended they were inflamed
As I was in reality inflamed

Perhaps all things can be told in a move
And a wrist turned is a poem
But a peasant is only a peasant
When she opens her mouth
It is then you experience the fact
That whilst her legs are excellent

She may have coarse emotions some of which
She owes to circumstances and some
Of which she employs wilfully to
Secure an advantage moving from one
To the other in the space of a sentence
Knowing this I breathed more easily

To the Aberystwyth Students

It is hard to get a hearing
And the educators lie willingly
And unwillingly
As do the poets

It is hard to get a hearing
And everything's sewn up
Sewn up as usual
But more sewn up than usual now

It is hard to get a hearing
But like the dew which falls in the dark
And the slow journey of rain through faults
The words seep down

Aberystwyth is so very chaste
Only Victory emerging from the dead
Looks flagrantly naked
But in such fractures it occurs

How far from the beat of mechanical
Art and oiled acting
How far from the centres where the
Secretaries yawn and discard their shoes

We gather round a text which yields
Meaning reluctantly
We try to perform the contradiction
We do not smooth and it occurs

That must be the purpose of art
That must be art occurring
Its discomfort is considerable
And yet we return